VOLLEYBALL

CONSULTANT

Robert E. Laveaga

REPRESENTING

The United States Volleyball Association

ATHLETIC INSTITUTE SERIES

STERLING PUBLISHING CO., INC.   New York

Foreword

This book on "Volleyball" is but one item in a comprehensive list of sports instruction aids made available on a non-profit basis by The Athletic Institute. The photographic material in this book has been reproduced in total from The Athletic Institute's sound, color slidefilm, "Beginning Volleyball." This book and the slidefilm are parts of a program designed to bring the many benefits of athletics, physical education, and recreation to everyone.

The Athletic Institute is a non-profit organization devoted to the advancement of athletics, recreation, and physical education. It functions on the premise that athletics and recreation bring benefits of inestimable value to the individual and to the community.

The nature and scope of the many Athletic Institute programs are determined by an advisory committee of selected persons noted for their outstanding knowledge, experience, and ability in the fields of athletics, recreation, and physical education.

It is their hope, and the hope of The Institute, that through this book, the reader will become a better volleyball player, skilled in the fundamentals of this fine game. Knowledge, and the practice necessary to mold knowledge into playing ability are the keys to real enjoyment of playing volleyball.

Copyright © 1962 by The Athletic Institute
Published by Sterling Publishing Co., Inc.
419 Fourth Avenue, New York 16, New York
Manufactured in the United States of America
Library of Congress Catalog Card No.: 62-12612

CONTENTS

DIAGRAM OF VOLLEYBALL COURTS

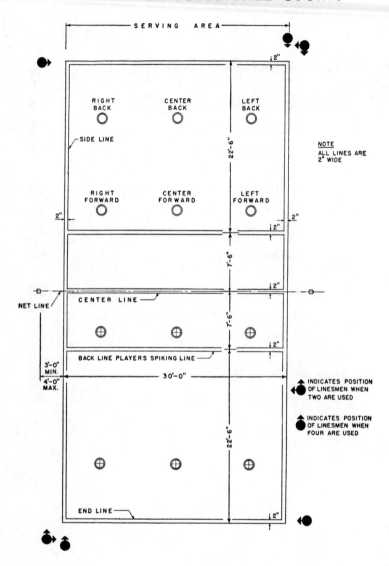

SERVING AREA

2"

RIGHT BACK CENTER BACK LEFT BACK

SIDE LINE

22'-6"

NOTE
ALL LINES ARE
2" WIDE

RIGHT FORWARD CENTER FORWARD LEFT FORWARD

2" 2" 2"

7'-6"

2"

NET LINE CENTER LINE 2"

7'-6"

2"

BACK LINE PLAYERS SPIKING LINE

3'-0" MIN.
4'-0" MAX.

30'-0"

INDICATES POSITION OF LINESMEN WHEN TWO ARE USED

INDICATES POSITION OF LINESMEN WHEN FOUR ARE USED

22'-6"

END LINE 2"

1

FUNDAMENTALS OF
VOLLEYBALL

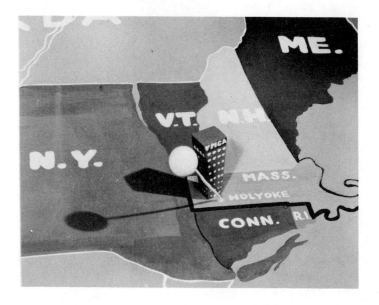

Eastern United States has been the birth-
place of two popular games that are en-
tirely American in origin. One was basket-
ball . . . the other, volleyball. In 1895, in
Holyoke, Massachusetts, William Morgan,
physical director of the local YMCA, in-
vented volleyball.

He intended the game to be a mild form of exercise and recreation for businessmen and in the beginning it was just that. The game consisted of batting a ball back and forth across a high net and the principal objective was to keep the ball in the air.

The ball was put in play with a service but there was no real vigor in it . . . just an easy lob across the net. But the game had merit . . .

. . . and the players soon recognized it. They started to play harder and develop skill, sensing the possibilities of an exciting, competitive sport. They changed the serve from an easy lob to a hard-driven ball . . .

. . . placing the ball accurately and strategically. As younger men and fine athletes joined the game, it began to develop into a spectacle of exciting and vigorous action.

And today volleyball is one of the most popular year-round sports. Age makes little difference because you can adjust the game's tempo to your mood, ability and skill.

Boys and girls can enjoy the game together because the skill of the game is as much agility and precision as pure strength.

And the seasons make no difference, either. It's just as much fun outdoors as inside. And those are the reasons why volleyball can be a life-long sport for you if you learn the fundamentals now.

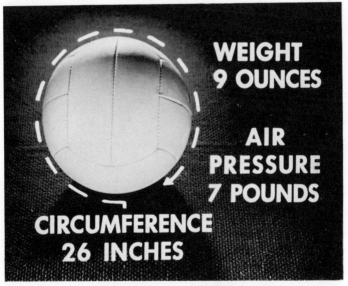

WEIGHT
9 OUNCES

AIR
PRESSURE
7 POUNDS

CIRCUMFERENCE
26 INCHES

The specifications of the original volleyball are still standard. It should weigh not less than nine ounces and not more than ten. Air pressure should be not less than seven pounds and not more than eight. Its circumference should be not less than twenty-six inches and not more than twenty-seven.

9

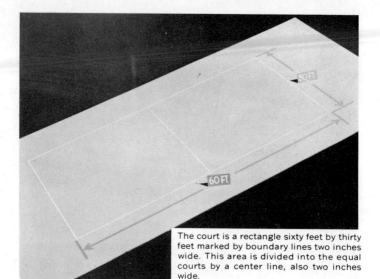

The court is a rectangle sixty feet by thirty feet marked by boundary lines two inches wide. This area is divided into the equal courts by a center line, also two inches wide.

The net across the center line is three feet in width, and the top should be eight feet from the floor. For women's and high school play, the net may be lowered.

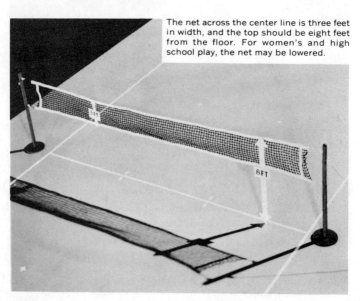

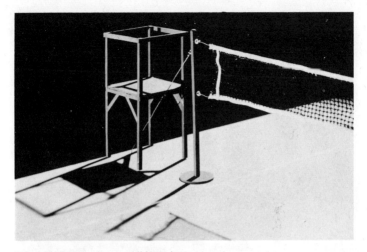

It is a good idea, when possible, to have a referee's platform constructed at one end of the net, elevated to a height of 4 feet, and large enough to support one man. If it is not possible to secure or make such a platform . . .

. . . the next best substitute is the old-fashioned step ladder. At any rate, the referee should be high enough to see the game without obstructions.

There are two recognized rule books for
volleyball . . . one approved by the United
States Volleyball Association and the
other approved by the Division for Girl's
and Women's Sports of the American
Association for Health, Physical Education,
and Recreation.

Each half of the court shall have a restrain-
ing line, which shall be 7½ feet from and
parallel to the middle of the center line.

There are six men on a volleyball team, and each man is responsible for covering the ground in one of the court areas. This division of the team places three men in the front half of the court and three in the rear.

These positions have designated names in relation to the court. They are left forward, center forward, right forward, right back, center back, and left back.

Now let's see how the game is played. We begin the game with the serve. The player in the right back position of the blue team goes to the serving zone, which is the area behind the end line.

The ball is put in play by the server, who stands behind the end line in the serving area. The server is not permitted to step on the end line until the ball has been served. After the ball leaves his hands, he is permitted to move into the court for play.

The service is made by hitting the ball with any part of the hand, fist or arm over the net and into the opponent's court.

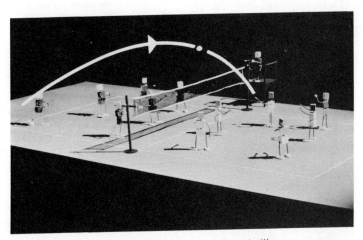

The served ball must go over the net without hitting it and land in the opponent's court.

If it goes out of bounds or hits any obstruction, or fails to clear the net, the serve is lost and no points are scored for either side.

The first man on the receiving team to receive the ball is known as number one.

His job is to pass the ball into the forward part of the court in such a manner that it will not be difficult for the next man, number two, to play it.

Number two is known as the set-up. His job is to set the ball up or hit it up close to, and above, the net on his own side, so that number three, the spiker or attack man, can hit it hard into the opponent's court.

When the set-up has been made, the spiker jumps into the air and hits the ball with a downward spiking motion so that it will be difficult for his opponents to return it.

Players are not allowed to touch the net or extend their hands over the net like this. However, no foul is declared if a player knocks the ball into the net, thus forcing it against, or under, an opposing player's hands.

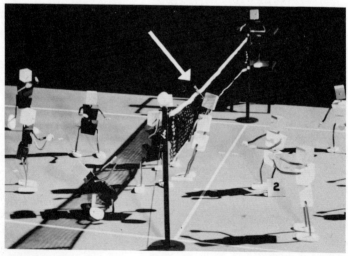

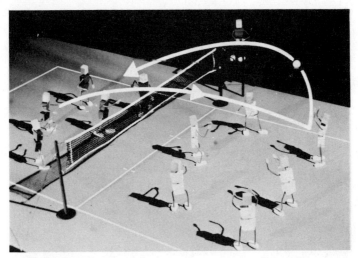

The first man to receive the ball on the receiving team may return it himself like this, but this makes for a slow, see-saw type of contest, instead of the hard, driving game that is much more fun to play.

Usually the other team will attempt to block the ball. Blocking may be done by any one or all of the opposing players, who leap high into the air, arms outstretched and try to break up the flight of the ball close to the net. The blocker who touches the ball first may send it back across the net; but for better accuracy . . .

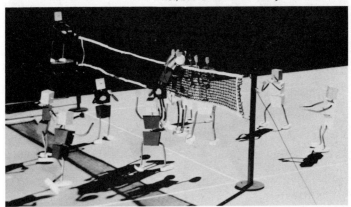

. . . he will deflect it upward and backward to one of his teammates in the rear, who will either return it himself, or send it forward to be hit over the net by one of his forward teammates.

The ball can be played only three times on each side of the net and no player may hit it twice in succession.

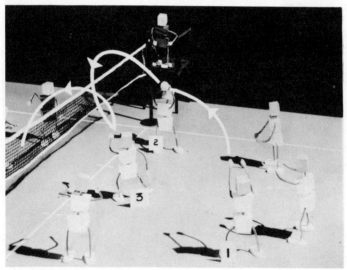

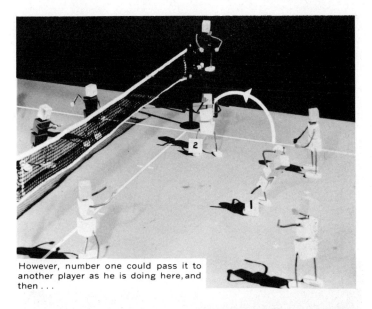

However, number one could pass it to another player as he is doing here, and then . . .

. . . have it returned to him and hit it again himself on the third play.

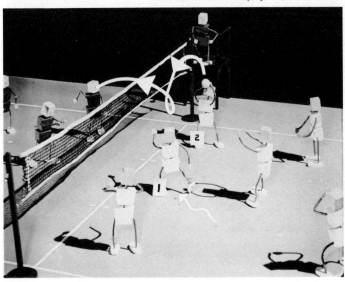

The basic rule of scoring is that only the
team that serves can score. In this respect
scoring is similar to badminton and table
tennis. Here, for instance, the white team
is serving.

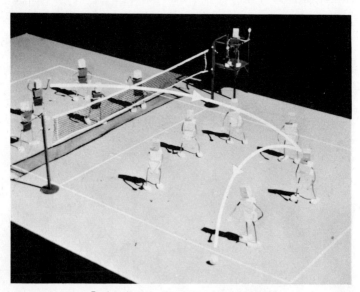

During the play the white team knocks the
ball out of bounds. The blue team does not
score. The white team simply loses the
service and the blue team gets the service.

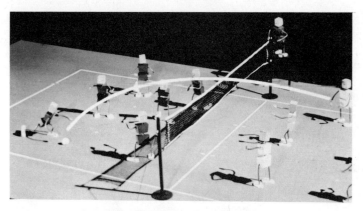

But here, during the white team's service, the blue team commits an error or a foul. In this case the white team scores one point, keeps the serve and continues to serve until it commits an error or foul.

During a game, whenever a team takes over the service, each player of that team rotates one position in a clockwise direction. The right forward moves back for the serve; the right back moves to the center back position, and so on. Then the man who moves into the service area will continue to serve until his team loses the service.

The team which loses the serve remains in position.

Players may overstep the side and back boundaries of the court to return a ball, and their feet may touch the center line, but not cross it.

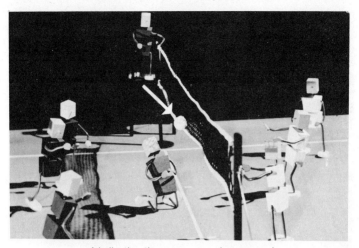

A ball, other than a serve, may be recovered from the net and kept in play provided the player avoids contact with the net and does not catch or hold the ball.

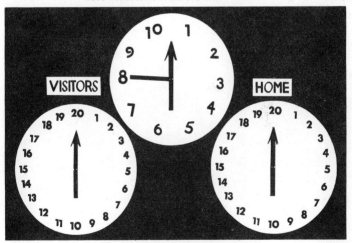

A game shall be won by the team that has scored the most points and is at least 2 points ahead:

    a. When one team has scored 15 points, or

    b. The first time the ball becomes dead after 8 minutes of ball-in-play, which ever occurs first.

If the leading team does not have a 2-point-advantage, unlimited overtime shall be played without interruption by any whistle or horn designating that the regular time has elapsed.

But supposing the game had gone to fourteen-fourteen. Now one team must score two points more than the other to win the game.

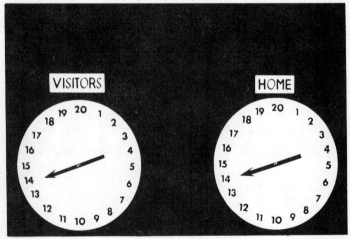

26

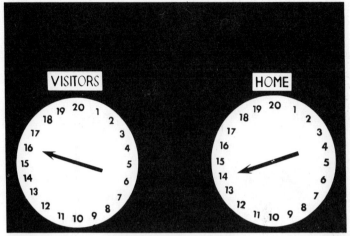

The visitors score two points and the game ends at sixteen-fourteen. When the score is tied at fourteen-all, one team must beat the other by two-points to win.

There are eight minutes of playing time in a game. If a team scores fifteen points before the eight minutes have expired and has a two-point advantage, that team wins and the game is ended. Here, after six minutes of play, the visitors have fifteen points and a two-point advantage, so they win 15-13.

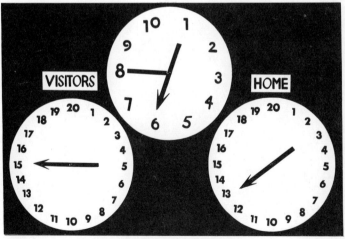

If, however, neither team scores fifteen points during the game period, the team with at least a two-point advantage wins and the game is ended. For instance, here at the end of eight minutes of play the score is twelve to ten for the visitors, so the visitors win. But if the score were 12-11 at the end of eight minutes, they would have to continue play until one team was two points ahead.

These are only the basic rules. To play well you should know them all and the best way to learn is to study the rule book. But no matter which rules you use, volleyball can be exciting and healthful.

This is the game that because of its inherent characteristics of fast action and keen competition, spread to the far corners of the globe to take its position among the most popular sports ever played—a favorite with men and women, young and old.

2

THE PASS

In volleyball as in every other sport, fun
increases with skill. From the very start,
you'll like the game, but the better you play,
the more you'll enjoy it.

So learning the fundamental skills is a worthwhile investment that pays off in real fun for many years. These fundamentals are not difficult to learn. All it takes is a little study of the basic movements and then plenty of practice.

Let's start by learning the fundamentals of the pass . . . how to pass the ball to the set-up when you are number one on the receiving team. Depending on where the ball comes to you, you will have to make your pass in a variety of positions.

You may have to take it high over your head . . .

. . . or out to the side, with one hand, if you can't reach it with both hands. The important thing is to get it up to your set-up man.

However, you'll have better control if you make every effort to get right underneath the ball and pass it with what is called a chest pass.

The chest pass is a simple movement of your hands from chest position upward to hit the ball sharply while your knees bend and straighten to add force and control to your pass. Let's analyze this movement.

First, the position of your hands on the ball. The ball should be played with your finger tips. If you let it come down into the palms of your hands you'll have difficulty controlling it. But if you hit it with your finger tips and keep your fingers stiff you'll get maximum power and good control.

The easiest way to get set for the chest pass is to raise your elbows sideways so that your upper arms are almost horizontal, pointing only slightly down from your shoulders. Keeping your elbows wide apart is the key to a successful pass.

34

Lower arms, wrists and hands should be a straight line . . . fingers spread and cupped with the thumbs pointing downward and slightly forward. From here . . .

. . . the chest pass is simply a forward and upward batting motion as you straighten your arms and thrust your finger tips forward to meet the ball. Practice this motion without the ball until it feels natural to you.

Now let's try it with the ball. Here's your stance during play . . . one foot forward, knees bent, body slightly forward with your weight up on the balls of your feet, ready to take the ball where it comes.

As the ball comes toward you, and you see you can take it with a chest pass, bring your hands up into the chest position. Now don't wait here for the ball. Your hands go out to meet it.

As the ball comes closer, bend your knees and at the same time extend your arms slightly toward the ball.

When the ball is almost to you, bring your hands back like a spring, ready to bounce forward and meet the ball.

Then when the ball is in the right position, straighten your elbows and strike the ball with the same batting action you practiced before. At the same time straighten your knees to bring your body upward and forward.

Contact the ball only with your finger tips, your fingers and wrists stiff up to this point. And now your wrists snap the ball forward.

38

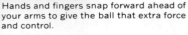
Hands and fingers snap forward ahead of your arms to give the ball that extra force and control.

And you end the pass with your hands and arms pointing in the direction of the pass, your weight well forward and up on the balls of your feet. That's the simple chest pass. Use it whenever you can, in preference to any other kind of pass

If the ball is high over your head, you may have to bend back at the waist to reach it, but even in this position, the fundamentals of the pass are the same.

To practice the chest pass, pass the ball back and forth between you and another player until you have the fundamentals well in mind and can execute them easily.

In today's volleyball, fast-moving and keenly competitive, most players use the chest pass whenever possible. But occasionally you just don't have time to get into position, and you have to pass a ball that's falling below your waist.

The best pass in this situation is what's known as the "dig"—a two-handed underhand pass that eliminates any chance of fouling by accidentally holding the ball. As the ball approaches, you're in a crouch position.

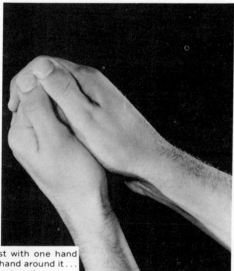

You've made a loose fist with one hand and wrapped your other hand around it . . . thumbs level on top, close together.

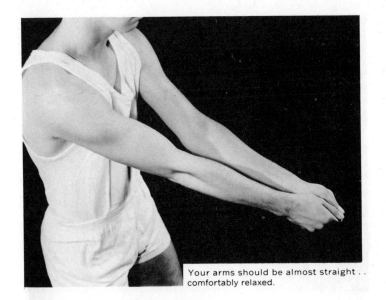

Your arms should be almost straight . .
comfortably relaxed.

Meet the ball with your wrists or forearms,
starting to lift up the instant the ball is
about to strike.

Keep your lifting action smooth and easy, with your arms moving from the shoulders and your legs straightening from a crouch in one continuous movement. The lift of the arms is only enough to carry "through the ball"—perhaps 8 to 10 inches. And it may be less if you're meeting a hard-driven spike. Your arms and wrists should stay relaxed, so you don't hit the ball too hard.

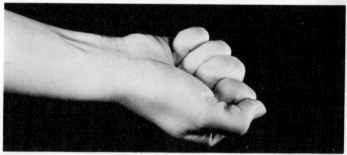

Some players make underhand passes with one fist instead of the regular dig. Keep your thumb next to the index finger to form an almost-flat surface, so you can meet the ball with your fingers and the fleshy part of your hand.

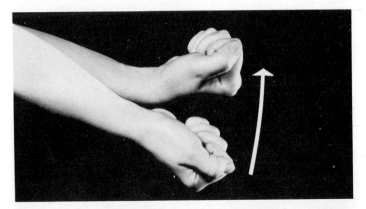

The blow with the closed fist is short and sharp, using both wrist and elbow as well as shoulder . . . just a quick upward snap of wrist, elbow, and shoulder as the ball reaches your hand.

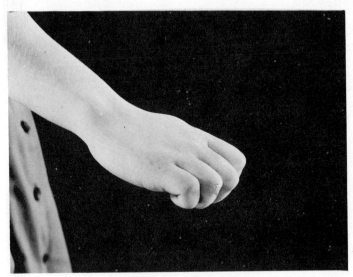

The back of the knuckles and wrist also may be used to hit low balls. Start by extending the hand and fingers in a straight line . . . then clench the fingers sharply at the first joint, to form an almost-flat surface.

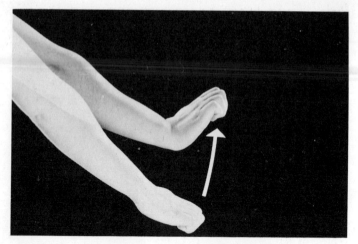

The striking movement is very similar to that of hitting with the clenched fist, except that the wrist snap is reversed. Arm and wrist are sharply snapped upward, and you hit the ball with the wrist and back knuckles.

Another way of making the underhand pass is the old "palms-up" method. While it's almost never used in today's tournament play, the method is still taught in some places. And if you're going to use it, you had better do it right . . . because there's always the risk of holding the ball. The waiting position is the same as in the dig pass . . .

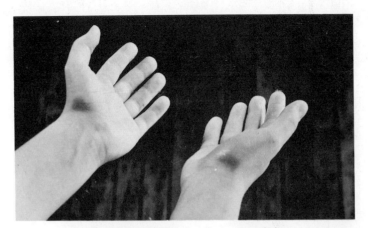

. . . except that your hands are extended
with the palms up. The fingers are almost
straight and held fairly flat. That's because
in this type of pass . . .

. . . you contact the ball only with the
fleshy parts of the fingers . . . not the
palms of your hands. As your fingers meet
the ball . . .

47

. . . your whole body quickly starts moving upward from the crouch position, starting with your knees and shoulders. But your fingers can be in contact with the ball for only an instant.

And the essential arm motion is a quick batting action . . . not lifting or throwing. The fingers contact the ball only long enough to bat it in the opposite direction.

But the easiest pass to control when you have to pass underhand is the dig. And it's a good method to use when you're recovering a ball hit into the net. When the ball hits the net, get under it as quickly as possible with your side to the net and your knees well bent. Wait for the ball to drop low. When you swing up with your lift, hit the ball high enough so a teammate can come under and drive it over the net.

The set-up is the action of the second player to handle the ball on the receiving team. The set-up's job is to pass the ball into such a position that a teammate can leap high near the net and drive it downward into the opposite court.

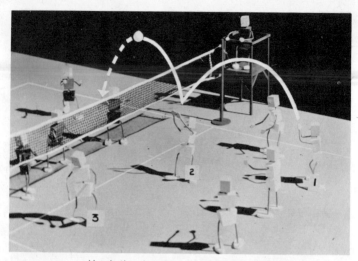

Here's the play with models. Number one takes the ball first and passes it forward to number two with a chest pass.

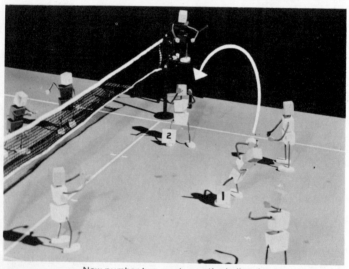

Now number two must pass the ball up in the air near and above the net so number three can leap up and hit the ball before it falls below the top of the net. Number two is called the set-up man.

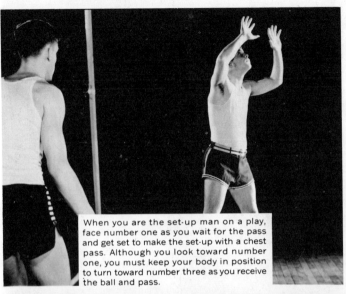

When you are the set-up man on a play, face number one as you wait for the pass and get set to make the set-up with a chest pass. Although you look toward number one, you must keep your body in position to turn toward number three as you receive the ball and pass.

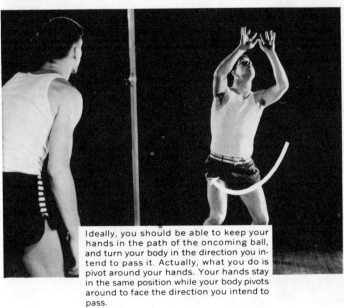

Ideally, you should be able to keep your hands in the path of the oncoming ball, and turn your body in the direction you intend to pass it. Actually, what you do is pivot around your hands. Your hands stay in the same position while your body pivots around to face the direction you intend to pass.

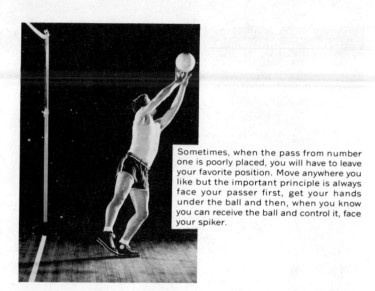

Sometimes, when the pass from number one is poorly placed, you will have to leave your favorite position. Move anywhere you like but the important principle is always face your passer first, get your hands under the ball and then, when you know you can receive the ball and control it, face your spiker.

When the pass comes to you very low, you may have to drop on one knee and bring the ball up with the dig pass.

But whenever you can, get under the ball for a chest pass. It's by far the most accurate pass for the set-up.

The height and distance from the net of your set-up should depend on the preference of the teammate who will spike it over the net. It can vary from two to ten feet above the net and from six to twenty inches away from the net.

Be sure to set up the ball in front of the attack as well as above him. Ideally, when you make your pass, the high point of the arc should be midway between you and your attack. With that kind of pass he can perform his spike with point-winning accuracy.

If you set it up behind the spiker like this, he will have to reach back and thus lose both power and accuracy.

The set-up is real team play. Spiking makes the points . . . but it's the set-up that makes the spike possible.

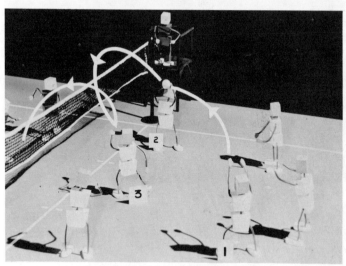

And a successful attack is the result of the cooperation of all three people—number one, the passer; number two, the set-up; and number three, the attack. So if you want to play winning volleyball, learn all three plays and practice them well.

The pass and the set-up are two of the most important team plays in volleyball. Without skill at both of these by every player on the team, winning volleyball is difficult. So learn them well and you'll find in this game the kind of fun that only fast, competitive play can bring.

3

THE SERVE

The serve puts the ball in play in volleyball, and since teams rotate the service during a game, every player must be able to serve well.

Originally the serve was not considered a point-making play. Its purpose was merely to get the ball over the net and start the volley. But gradually a faster, harder serve was developed as a scoring play, and today, more and more players are changing from the easy, underhand serve . . .

. . . to the overhand, or power serve. But the overhand serve requires more skill, and it takes consistent practice to make the power serve accurate.

In either serve, certain basic rules must be observed. The server must stand behind the back boundary line.

The ball must go over the net without touching the net or any other object and must land either on or inside the boundary lines.

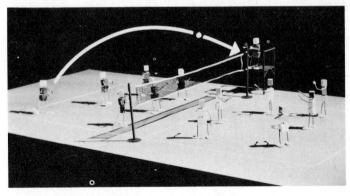

Let's analyze the basic movements of the serve. Since the underhand is the basic, beginning serve, let's learn it first.

There is the complete movement. You simply hold the ball in your left hand, swing your right hand back behind you, then bring it forward and bat the ball off your left hand with an upward motion. Let's try it first without the ball.

First, foot position. If you're right-handed, your left foot should be forward a little, facing front, with knees relaxed.

Now pretend you are holding a ball in your left hand just a little in front of your right hip . . . your left arm close to your body. Now the backswing with your right arm.

It's a full body movement. Your right knee bends forward and your whole body pivots around to the right as your right arm swings back and upward. Keep your eye on the ball.

At the end of your backswing you should be able to feel the pull in your arm muscles as your arm starts its sweep downward. Your body starts the downswing as you twist to the left and start your hand swinging toward the ball.

As your right hand meets your left, your knees are still bent, holding back the power of your legs for the final batting action.

Then straighten your legs, arch your back, put the final ounce of power into your swing and follow through easily and naturally. That's all there is to it. Now, let's try it with the ball.

There's your stance. Ball in your left hand, just in front of your right hip . . . your left arm close to your body. Throughout the serve try to keep your left elbow close to your body. It will help you control your serve.

As you start your backswing, bend your knees, your weight coming back on your rear foot, but keep the ball in about the same position by keeping approximately the same bend in your left elbow.

As the downswing starts, your weight moves forward again, your body and shoulders twist around to the left and your arm starts its arc down toward the ball.

As your hand nears the ball its swing has started upward.

65

Hit the ball with the heel of your hand, your palm and your fingers, simply knocking it off your left hand.

Now your knees start to straighten and you start to arch your back, putting all your power into the serve as the ball leaves your left hand.

And you follow through easily and naturally as your right hand swings on upward and your left swings off to the side for balance.

Practice this underhand serve over and over until the whole movement feels easy and natural, and you are able to serve accurately.

When the simple underhand is familiar to you, it will be time to practice putting a twist, or "English" on your serve. It makes the ball spin as it travels and your opponents will have more trouble handling it.

The fundamentals for the curve serve are exactly the same up to this point, when your hand contacts the ball. Instead of hitting it directly behind and a little underneath as in the straight underhand, you hit it a little on the right side. And you hit with the palm and fingers rather than the palm and heel.

Let your hand roll up the ball as you hit it.

And rotate your arm and hand inward, over the top of the ball, as you make your delivery. If this blow has enough force, it will spin the ball to the left and curve it toward the left boundary of your opponent's court. This is called an "out" curve.

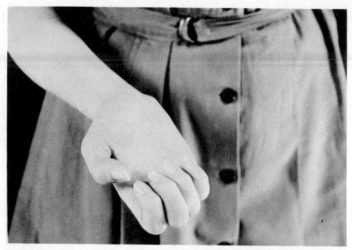

If you deliver an underhand serve with your hand in this position you will have what is called a "floater" or "knuckle ball," a deceptive serve that is hard to handle. The fundamental movements are the same except . . .

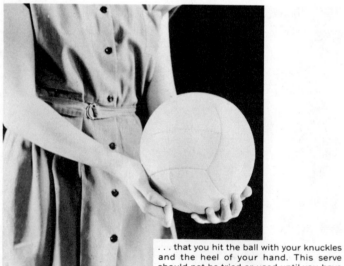

. . . that you hit the ball with your knuckles and the heel of your hand. This serve should not be tried or used until you have mastered the basic underhand service.

After you have the underhand serve under control, both sexes will want to try the more powerful and effective overhand. The fundamental techniques are not difficult. You can learn them quickly. But you'll probably need practice for accuracy.

The serve consists simply of tossing the ball in the air, higher than your head, and batting it forward with an overarm swing like a catcher's throw in baseball. It's much like the service in tennis.

Start by standing facing the court squarely. You may vary this position to suit yourself as you develop skill, but facing the court squarely is a good starting position.

Your left foot should be slightly ahead of the right with about ten inches between your heels to give you a good solid base for action.

Hold the ball in both hands about waist high. Now the first movement is in your knees. Drop your hips by bending your knees . . . but hold the ball steady.

Then push upward with your knees and start tossing the ball upward with both hands. Keep your body upright.

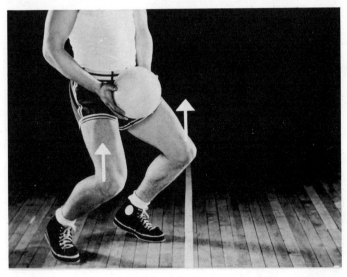

Toss the ball upwards to a height of not more than five feet above you. If you throw it any higher, it will gain so much momentum during the long, downward drop that it will be hard to hit accurately. As the ball leaves your hands, keep your right hand swinging backward.

As the ball starts down hold your arm back, forearm upright and upper arm horizontal, waiting to time your forward swing.

Keep your eye on the ball all the way up and down because timing is the essence of this serve.

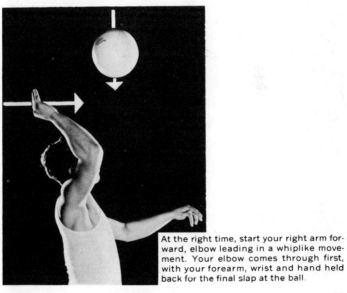

At the right time, start your right arm forward, elbow leading in a whiplike movement. Your elbow comes through first, with your forearm, wrist and hand held back for the final slap at the ball.

75

Then your arm straightens as your wrist and hand whip forward toward the ball.

Just before you contact the ball your wrist is still laid back, ready to snap forward at the instant of contact. And your whole body is pivoting around to the left with the force of your swing.

Hit the ball with your hand cupped, palm and fingers contacting the ball. And now whip your hand forward on your wrist in a final wrist snap.

And follow through after the ball with your weight forward, your right arm swinging forward and downward. That's the overhand serve. Learn the technique and practice it faithfully and you'll find you can play better volleyball.

A popular variation of the overhand serve is the floater, delivered with the right hand in the same position as in an underhand floater . . . fingers doubled sharply under at the first knuckles.

All the fundamentals are the same except that you toss the ball slightly forward and not very high.

Then hit the ball with the heel of your hand and your knuckles. You should hit it dead center or slightly above center . . . not below center.

Then the same wrist snap and follow through. The "floater" is a useful serve for deception; but it should be tried only after you have control and power with the basic overhand.

Without a good serve, either underhand or overhand, you cannot play winning volleyball. Learn first the underhand; then the overhand; then the variations; and you'll find your fun from the game increasing as your own skill improves.

79

4

THE ATTACK

The attack is not only the most colorful and spectacular play in volleyball—it is your best point-maker. Sometimes called the spike, it is the third and final play of the ball on the three-man offense.

The set-up man takes a pass from number one; then sets it up for the attacker or spiker . . .

. . . who leaps high in the air to reach the ball before it falls below the top of the net and drives it into the opposite court. The attack is an energetic play.

The sustained jumping and the strain of the movement requires stamina, alertness and, above all, a sturdy pair of legs.

Therefore, you'd be wise to take frequent leg exercises such as skipping rope and running on your toes.

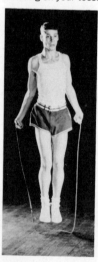

The attack is a coordinated movement of arms and legs that will require considerable practice. Let's study the arm movement first.

Throughout most of the movement your elbow leads in a whiplike movement that lets the forearm, wrist and hand lay back until the final slap at the ball. On the start of the upswing the elbow starts up first.

Then when the elbow reaches its highest point, the forearm and hand continue on up; then suddenly reverse the direction and slap downward.

But the elbow stays high until after the ball is hit. Before the follow-through, only the forearm and hand move downward, and you should feel the move in your shoulder muscles as your arm rotates on your shoulder joint.

Try that movement with a ball. Hold the ball in your left hand about waist high and prepare to slap the ball downward using that same whiplike action.

The elbow starts up first; your hand should trail like the end of a cracking whip. When your elbow comes about even with the top of your head . . .

. . . your forearm continues on up until it is about perpendicular. Now your arm starts rotating on your shoulder joint . . .

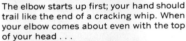

. . . and you slap the ball downward. At this point, just as your hand touches the ball, your wrist should snap downward. It's a whipping, slapping motion with its greatest force just as you contact the ball.

Although the ball may be hit with the fist or the heel of the hand, it's best to start by using your cupped hand. This way a beginning player will have more control.

Now, in order to get the feel of that slapping movement while you're in the air, try the same thing as you jump into the air with the ball. At the height of your jump . . .

86

. . . slap the ball downward with all your strength. Practice this until you can bounce the ball high into the air with the force of your blow. Then you're ready to coordinate this arm movement with the footwork of the approach or take-off of the attack

Here is the footwork alone. Let's try it without arm movement. In a game you'll take any number of steps you need, but to learn the fundamentals, we'll take a three-step approach. Stand about five feet from the net, facing diagonally toward the net, in a normal playing position. Now the first move is with your left foot.

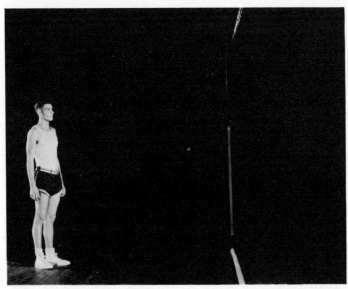

A snort step forward with the left foot . . . not a long step. You have three steps to reach the net so judge your distances accordingly.

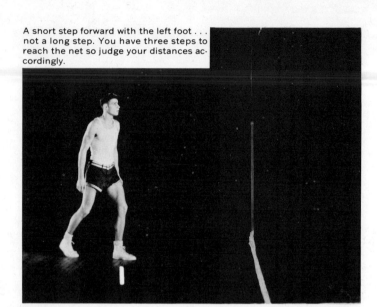

Then a step with the right foot . . .

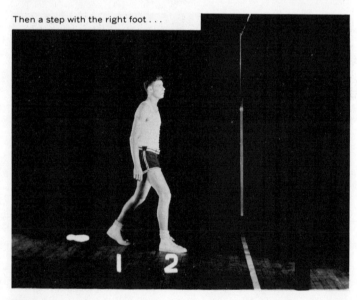

. . . and another step with the left. This brings you up to the net and your next movement is to get into position for your jump.

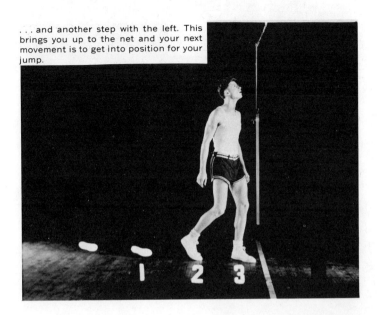

As you crouch for the jump, bring your right foot up even with the left and leap. There's the footwork of the approach . . . a four-count movement that ends with your body crouched, ready to leap. Practice that footwork alone for a while . . . then try coordinating it with the arm movement you've already learned. Here it is.

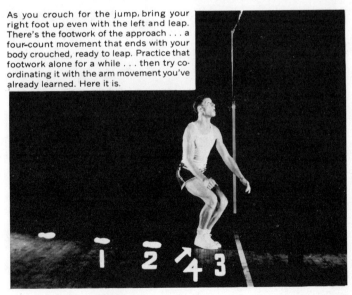

89

As you start forward with your left foot on the first count, your arms are at your sides and ready. Keep them there until . . .

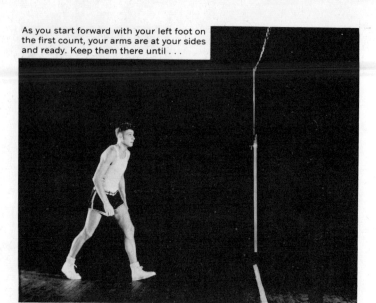

. . . as your right foot comes down on the second count, your right arm starts back. It stays back until . . .

. . . the fourth count when you start your leap. Then it starts forward and upward with your leap.

Both arms swing upward during your leap, adding the force of your swinging arms to the push with your legs, until . . .

. . . at the height of your jump, your arm is extended upward, ready to start down.

Then, as the ball comes into position, use the slapping movement you learned earlier, hitting on top of the ball to spike it downward. This spiking movement will carry your body around to the left in your follow-through . . .

. . . and you land facing the net with both feet spread. Now let's try that arm and leg coordination in actual playing conditions.

Have a set-up man stand near the net and toss the ball about three feet above the net and a little in front of you. Your approach should start just as he starts the set-up.

The exact timing of your take-off is a matter of practice. You should practice with your set-up man frequently and consistently until your timing becomes automatic.

Approach the net with your left side to the net, if you are right-handed . . . right side to the net if you play left-handed.

During your leap your left side remains
toward the net . . .

. . . but during the spike your body twists
around until you are facing the net . . .

. . . and you land with feet spread, facing the net, ready for the next play. That's the complete attack movement. There are many variations of it but before trying any of them you should learn these basic fundamentals and practice them until your rhythm and timing are automatic.

Then you'll find the fun of volleyball is increased many times. The spike is the winning play of volleyball.

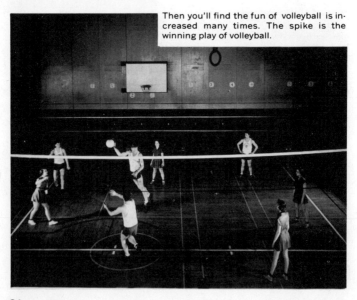